SUNDAY SOUTHERN FAVORITES

VOLUME ONE

12 Easy-to-Perform Gospel Favorites

Arranged and Orchestrated by
MARTY HAMBY

lillenas
PUBLISHING COMPANY
lillenas.com

Copyright © 2019 by Lillenas Publishing Company, Box 419527, Kansas City, MO 64141. All rights reserved.
Litho in U.S.A.

CONTENTS

When I Wake Up to Sleep No More 3

I Never Shall Forget the Day 18

Where Could I Go 32

The Unseen Hand *with* Leaning on the Everlasting Arms . . . 43

I Can Call Jesus Anytime 59

Better Hurry Up 72

I Can't Even Walk (Without You Holding My Hand) 84

I'm Standing on the Solid Rock 99

I Won't Have to Worry Anymore 110

Touring That City 119

My God Is Real 134

That I Could Still Go Free 147

When I Wake Up to Sleep No More

3

Words and Music by
MARION W. EASTERLING
Arranged by Marty Hamby

Rockabilly (♩ = 180)

What a glad thought some won-der-ful

Copyright © 1944 Bridge Building Music (BMI) (adm. at CapitolCMGPublishing.com).
All rights reserved. Used by permission.
PLEASE NOTE: The copying of this music is prohibited by law and is not covered by CCLI or OneLicense.net.

morn-ing just to hear Ga-briel's trum-pet sound, when I wake

when I wake up to sleep no more.
up to sleep no more.

Ris-ing to meet our bless-ed Re-deem-er with a glad

19
shout I'll leave the ground, when I wake
when I wake up
C♯m B E
22
2
up to sleep no more.
to sleep no more.
When I wake
C♯m B7 E B C♯m7 B/D♯
25
Some glad morn - ing, jew - els a -
up to sleep no more,
E F♯m/E E

dorning, o-ver in glo-ry, happy I'll be on heav-en's bright

tell-ing the sto-ry, With the re-deemed of all the a-
shore.

-ges, prais-ing the One whom I a-dore, when I wake

when I __ wake up to sleep no more. __
up to sleep no more. __

Glo-ry to God, I'll have a new

48
bod - y, changed in the twin-kling of an eye,
when I wake
Bb/F F Dm C F
51
when I wake up to sleep no more. Leav-ing be -
up to sleep no more. Leav-ing be -
F G7 C
55
hind all trou-ble and sor - row, bound for that cit - y up on high,
F Bb/F F Dm C

when I___ wake up to sleep no
when I___ wake up to sleep no

F   Dm C7

more.   Some glad
When I___ wake up

F   F

morn-ing,   jew-els a-dorn-ing,
to sleep no more,   hap-py I'll

Gm/F F   Gm/F F

o - ver in glo - ry, tell - ing the
be on heav - en's bright shore.
sto - ry, With the re - deemed of all the a - ges, prais - ing the
One whom I a - dore,___ when I__ wake
when I__ wake up

up to sleep no more.

When I ___ wake

Dm C7 F

Some glad morn-ing, jew-els a-
up to sleep no more,

F Gm/F F

dorn-ing, o-ver in glo-ry,
hap-py I'll be on heav-en's bright

Gm/F F Gm/F F

tell - ing the sto - ry, With the re - deemed of all the a-
shore.

C7 F

- ges, prais - ing the One whom I a - dore,___ when I___ wake

Gm/F F Dm C F

when I___ wake up,___   when I___ wake
up,   when I___ wake up,

C/E Dm F/C

13

up, when I ___ wake up   to sleep no

Bb   F/C   C7

more! _____

F   N.C.   F

Glo-ry to God, I'll have a new

Bb/C   F

body, changed in the twin-kling of an eye,___ when I___ wake

when I___ wake up to sleep no more. Leav-ing be-
up to sleep no more. Leav-ing be-

hind all trou-ble and sor-row, bound___ for that cit - y up on high,___

15

when I___ wake up to sleep no
when I___ wake up   to sleep no

F   Dm   C7

more.   Some   glad
When I___ wake up

F   F

morn-ing,   jew-els a-dorn-ing,
to sleep no more,   hap-py I'll

Gm/F   F   Gm/F F

16

o - ver in glo - ry, tell - ing the
be on heav-en's bright shore.

sto - ry, With the re - deemed of all the a - ges, prais - ing the

One whom I a - dore, when I wake
when I wake up,

up, when I wake up, when I wake up
when I wake up, when I wake up

to sleep no more!

I Never Shall Forget the Day

Words and Music by
G. T. SPEER
Arranged by Marty Hamby

Country pop (♩ = 148)

ALTO SOLO

Long years a- go, when out in sin,

Copyright © 1965 Ben Speer Music (SESAC) (adm. at ClearBox Rights, LLC).
All rights reserved. Used by permission.
PLEASE NOTE: The copying of this music is prohibited by law and is not covered by CCLI or OneLicense.net.

19

I had no hope, no peace with- in. Down on my knees in ag-o-ny, I prayed to Jesus and He gladly set me free.

(ALTO SOLO)
22
f
I nev - er shall for - get the
CHOIR parts
f
I nev - er shall
f
N.C.
G
G/D
Am/D
G
G/D
f
25
day when all the bur - dens from my
for - get the day, bur - dens, my
G
G/D
Am/D
G
G/D
Am/G
G
G/D

28
soul were rolled_ a - way. It made me
soul were rolled, rolled a - way.___
Am/G G A7 D D/A C/D
31
hap - py, glad, and free, I'll sing and
It made me hap - py, hap - py, glad, and free,
G G/D Am/D G G/D G G/B C G G/D C/D

shout it, for He's ev-'ry-thing to me.

Shout it, for He's ev-'ry-thing.

Oh, sin-ner

come to Je-sus now, At His dear

feet just hum-bly bow. Con-fess to

24

Him your ev-'ry sin, He'll save and cleanse you, give you peace and joy within.

Oo__ Oh Ah

12

25

soul were rolled a-way. It made me
soul were rolled, rolled a-way.

hap - - - py, glad, and free,
It made me hap-py, hap-py, glad, and

I'll sing and shout it, for He's ev-'ry-thing to me.

free, Shout it, for He's ev-'ry-thing.

I nev-er shall

I nev-er

Drums

for - get the day when all the

shall for - get the day,

bur - dens from my soul were rolled a - way.

bur - dens, my soul were rolled, rolled a - way.

It made me hap - - py, glad, and

It made me hap - py,

free, I'll sing and shout it, for He's

hap - py, glad, and free, Shout it, for He's

ev-'ry-thing to me. I'll sing and

ev-'ry-thing.

shout it, for He's ev-'ry-thing to me.

Shout it, for He's ev-'ry-thing.

A | A/C♯ Bm/D | A/E D/E | N.C.

Ev - 'ry - thing _____ to me! _____

Ev - 'ry - thing to me! _____

Where Could I Go

Words and Music by
JAMES B. COATS
Arranged by Marty Hamby

com - fort can af - ford.

striv - ing a - lone to face temp - ta - tions sore,

where could I go but to the Lord?

Where could I go?

O where could I go, seek-ing a ref-uge for my soul?

29
Need - ing a friend to
C7 A♭m/C Gm/C F Am/C F7 F7/A
32
save me in the end,
Broth - er, won't you tell me
B♭ Gm/B♭ F F/A B♭/D
34
where could I go but to the Lord?
F F7/A Gm/B♭ F/C Dm/C C7

36
17
MEN unis.
mp
Neigh - bors are kind,
F7 F7/A B♭ B♭6/D F C♭/D♭ G♭ B♭m/D♭
mp
39
I love them ev - 'ry one,
G♭7 G♭7/B♭ C♭ A♭m/C♭ G♭ G♭/D♭ D♭7sus
42
Add LADIES
We get a - long in sweet ac - cord;
mel.
G♭ G♭/D♭ A♭m/D♭ G♭ A♭m/G♭ G♭ D♭ A♭7
3

But when my soul needs man-na from a-bove, where could I go but to the Lord?

Where could I go? O where could I go, seeking a refuge for my soul? Needing a friend

to save me in the end, where could I go

Brother, won't you tell me where could I go but to the Lord?

Where could I go? O where could I go, seeking a refuge for my soul, for my soul?

Need-ing a friend to save me in the end, Broth-er, won't you tell me Where could I go? Where could I go?

Where could I go___ but to the___ Lord,_____ to the Lord!___

The Unseen Hand
with Leaning on the Everlasting Arms

Words and Music by
RUPERT CRAVENS and **DANIEL J. COCKERHAM**
Arranged by Marty Hamby

43

MALE SOLO

There is an un -

Copyright © 1972 Bridge Building Music (BMI) (adm. at CapitolCMGPublishing.com).
All rights reserved. Used by permission.

PLEASE NOTE: The copying of this music is prohibited by law and is not covered by CCLI or OneLicense.net.

-seen hand to me, That leads through ways I cannot see; While going through this world of

45

(MALE SOLO)

woe, This hand still leads me as I go. I'm trusting to

CHOIR parts
I'm trusting to

the un - seen hand, that guides me the un - seen hand, that guides me

Am/F# | B7/D# | Em | G7/D | C | Am7

through this wear - y land; through this wear - y land;

G | Bm7/F# | Em7 | A7 | Am7

And some sweet day I'll reach that strand, Still guid-ed by

And some sweet day I'll reach that strand, Still guid-ed by

40
the unseen hand.
the unseen hand.
G/B Am/C G/D D7 G G7/B
mp
23
43
mf
I long to see
C E♭7 D♭/E♭ A♭ B♭m/A♭
mf

my Sav-ior's face, And sing the sto - - - ry "Saved by Grace", "Saved by

And there up-on that Gold-en Grace", There up-on that Strand, I'll praise Him for Gold-en Strand, I'll praise Him

His guid - ing hand. I'm trust - ing
for His guid - ing hand. I'm trust - ing

to the un - seen hand,
to the un - seen hand,

that guides me through this wear-y

that guides me through this wear-y

land; And some sweet day

land; And some sweet day

*Leaning on the Everlasting Arms

* Words by Elisha Hoffman / Music by Anthony J. Showalter
Arr. © 2019 PsalmSinger Music (BMI) (admin. by Music Services). All rights reserved.

ing, lean - ing, Safe and se - cure from all a - larms. I'm trust - ing I'm trust - ing

55

land; And some sweet land, wear-y land; day I'll reach that strand, Some sweet day I'll reach that strand,

Still guid-ed by, I'm lean-in' on the Ev-er-last-ing

Still guid-ed by, Lean-in' on the

Arms, and I'm hold-in'

Ev-er-last-ing arms. I'm holding

on to God's un - seen hand. His un - seen hand!

on to God's un - seen hand. His un - seen hand!

I Can Call Jesus Anytime

Words and Music by
BROCK SPEER
Arranged by Marty Hamby

Gospel shuffle (♩=128)

Copyright © 1955, renewed 1983 Ben Speer Music (SESAC) (adm. at ClearBox Rights, LLC). All rights reserved. Used by permission.
PLEASE NOTE: The copying of this music is prohibited by law and is not covered by CCLI or OneLicense.net.

I can call Jesus anytime. When I feel discouraged, He will lead me on, You know, I can call

28
18
SOP. f You know
Je - sus an - y - time.
G7 C7 F B♭ F
21
I can call Je - sus an - y -
f I can call Je - sus, I can call Je - sus,
F B♭/F F/C F B♭/F F/C
23
time, yes, I can. You know
Call Him an - y - time, call Him an - y - time. You know
F Dm/F F/C F Dm/F F/C

He, He is always on the line. He is King Almighty, Lord God is His Name. You know, I can call

Je - sus__ an - y - time.__

MEN *unis.* When the__ storm is rag - ing__

LADIES unis.
CHOIR parts
43
mf
You know, I can call
and the bil - lows roll,
F
Dm
F
46
Je - sus any - time.
G7
C
G7/D
C
LADIES unis.
49
mf
When my heart is heav-y and my spir - it's
F
F/C
F
F/C
F

52
CHOIR parts
low, You know, I can call Je - sus an - y -
Dm B♭ F/C Dm Dm7 G7 C7
55
30
time.
f
You know I can call
I can call Je - sus,
F B♭ F F B♭/F F/C
58
Je - sus an - y - time, yes, I
I can call Je - sus, Call Him an - y - time,
F B♭/F F/C F Dm/F F/C

60
can. You know He, He is
call Him an - y - time. You know He, He is
F Dm/F F/C F Dm7
62
al - ways on the line.
G7 C G7/D C7
65
He is King Al - might-y, Lord God is His
F F/C F F/C F

Name._ You know, I____ can call Jesus__ any-time.____

Dm B♭ F/C Dm Dm7 G7 C7

LADIES unis. *mp*
Well, I___ can call Jesus,

MEN unis. *mp*
I__ can call Jesus,

F F7/A B♭ B♭6/D F

Yes, I___ can call Jesus. I__

F

Add LADIES
76
mf
can call Je - sus. I can call Je - sus,
mf
G♭
mf
78
I can call Je - sus!
G♭
A♭m
G♭
G♭
C♭
D♭
80
f You know I can call
You know I can call Je - sus,
f
D♭7sus
G♭
C♭
G♭
G♭
D♭
f

69

89
32
He is King Al-might-y, Lord God is His
G♭ G♭/D♭ G♭ G♭/D♭ G♭
92
Name. You know, I can call Je-sus an-y-
E♭m C♭ G♭/D♭ E♭m E♭m7 A♭7 D♭7
95
time. You know,
G♭ G♭/B♭ C♭6 C♭6/E♭ G♭ C♭

I _____ can call Jesus _____ an-y-time, _____ an-y-time! _____

Better Hurry Up

Words and Music by
JAMES B. PARIS
Arranged by Marty Hamby

Rockabilly (♩ = 184)

CHOIR *parts*

Christ has gone, a home to pre-pare,

Copyright © 1941 Bridge Building Music (BMI) (adm. at CapitolCMGPublishing.com). All rights reserved. Used by permission.
PLEASE NOTE: The copying of this music is prohibited by law and is not covered by CCLI or OneLicense.net.

up be-yond the blue sky. It must be so wondrous-ly fair, nev-er seen by mor-tal eye. We know soon He's com-ing a-gain from His heav-en-ly throne. We shall leave this earth-ly do - main when He comes to claim His own. You bet-ter hur-ry up, get read-y to go. You bet-ter

hur - ry up, no time to be slow. If you want to ride on the glo - ry cloud with the Sav - ior and His cho - sen crowd, you bet - ter hur - ry up, get read - y to go.

LADIES *unis.*
Give your heart to Je - sus to - day.

77

LADIES parts

Oh, why long-er ref-use? Let Him wash your sins all a-way. He's the on-ly one to choose.

MEN unis.

Do not wait un-til it's too late; Let Him be your true

guide. Enter in at mercy's bright gate. It is standing open wide. You better hurry up, get ready to go. You better hur - ry up, no time to be slow. If you want to ride on the glo - ry cloud with the Sav - ior and His cho - sen crowd, you bet - ter

G G/D G A7 D G G/D G7 C

hur - ry up, get read - y to go.

You bet - ter hur - ry up,

get read - y to go. You bet - ter hur - ry up,

no time to be slow. If you want to ride on the glo-ry cloud with the Sav-ior and His cho-sen crowd, you bet-ter hur-ry up,

82

get read-y to go. You bet-ter hur-ry up, hur-ry up, hur-ry up, hur-ry up, hur-ry up, hur-ry up, hur-ry up, hur-ry up, hur-ry up, hur-ry up, hur - ry up, hur - ry up,

get read - y to go.

You bet - ter hur - ry up!

I Can't Even Walk
(Without You Holding My Hand)

Words and Music by
COLBERT CROFT and JOYCE CROFT
Arranged by Marty Hamby

Soulfully (♩. = 62)

MALE SOLO

I thought num - ber

Copyright © 1975 Curb Dayspring Music (BMI) (adm. at Warner-Tamerlane Publishing Corp). All rights reserved. Used by permission.
PLEASE NOTE: The copying of this music is prohibited by law and is not covered by CCLI or OneLicense.net.

one would sure - ly be me, I thought I could be what I want - ed to be. I thought I could build on life's sink - ing sand, but I can't e - ven walk with-out You hold-ing my hand.

I thought I could do a

87

man, but I can't e - ven walk with-out You hold-ing my hand.

I

CHOIR *parts*

I

43
can't e - ven walk with-out You hold - ing my
can't e - ven walk with-out You hold - ing my
C♭
A♭m/C♭
G♭
A♭m/G♭
f
46
hand, The moun-tain's too high and the
hand, the moun-tain's too high and the
G♭
A♭7
D♭
G♭/D♭
D♭
C♭/D♭
D♭

val-ley's too wide. Down on my val-ley's too wide. Down on my knees, I learned to stand, Lord, I knees, I learned to stand, I

55
can't e - ven walk_ with-out_ You hold-ing my
can't e - ven walk__ with-out_ You hold-ing my
G♭/D♭ G♭/B♭ A♭m/C♭ G♭/D♭ A♭m/D♭ B♭m/D♭ A♭m/D♭
58
42
hand.
hand.
G♭ G♭/B♭ Am7

MALE SOLO

I think I'll make Jesus my all in all, and if I'm in trouble, on His Name I'll call. If

70
I did - n't trust Him, I'd be less of a
CHOIR parts
mf
Oo
Ah
mf
G
Am/C
B7
73
man, but I can't e - ven walk with-out You
I can't e - ven walk with-out You
C
A7(no3)/C♯
G/D
G/B
Am/C
G/D

43
76
holding my hand.
I
Am/D Bm/D Am/D G G7 F6/A G7/B
79
can't even walk without You holding my
C Dm/C C Am/C G Am/G

95

(SOLOIST may ad lib)

hand, The moun-tain's too high and the

hand, the moun-tain's too high and the

val-ley's too wide, Down on my

val-ley's too wide. Down on my

knees, I learned to stand. Lord, I
knees, I learned to stand, I
can't e-ven walk without You hold-ing my
can't e-ven walk without You hold-ing my

hand. Lord, I can't e - ven
hand. I can't e - ven

walk without You hold - - ing my
walk without You hold - - ing my

98

I'm Standing on the Solid Rock

Words and Music by
HAROLD LANE
Arranged by Marty Hamby

Tenderly, with emotion (♩ = 94)

Through my dis-ap-point-ments, strife and dis-con-tent-ment, I cast my ev-'ry care on the Lord. No

Copyright © 1977 Ben Speer Music (SESAC) (adm. at ClearBox Rights, LLC). All rights reserved. Used by permission.
PLEASE NOTE: The copying of this music is prohibited by law and is not covered by CCLI or OneLicense.net.

mat-ter what ob-ses-sion, pain or deep de-pres-sion, I'm stand-ing on the sol-id

46 **Gospel Shuffle** (♩ = 188)

I'm stand-ing on the rock. I'm stand-ing on the rock,

Gospel Shuffle (♩ = 188)

25
rock of a - ges, Safe from all the
on the rock of a - ges, Safe from ev - 'ry storm,
F F/C F Gm/F F C C/G C B♭/C C7
29
storm that rag - es. Rich but not from
all the storm that rag - es. Rich in love, I'm rich,
F F/C F Gm/F F/C F F/C F Gm/F F/C Gm/C
33
Sa - tan's wag - es, I'm stand - ing on the sol - id
not from Sa - tan's wag - es, I'm stand - ing on the sol - id
F F/C F/C C♯°7 Dm F/C F/A Gm/B♭ F/C C7

102

37 rock. *Smoother*

rock.   TENORS *only* Ev-en though He's gone now,

41 I don't feel a-lone now, With com-fort came the Spir-it of the

45 Lord.   BASSES *only* Now with His Word to guide me, from temp-ta-tions hide me, I'm standing on the sol-id rock.

I'm stand-ing on the rock. I'm stand-ing on the rock, rock of a-ges, Safe

on the rock of a-ges, Safe from ev-'ry

104

rock. Now I'm press-ing on-ward, each step leads me home-ward, I'm trust-ing in my Sav-ior day by day. And close is our re-la-tion, firm is its foun - da - tion, So on this sol - id rock I'll

CHOIR *parts*

Oh, yes, I'm stand - ing on the stay. Oh, yes, I'm stand-ing on the rock,

rock of a - ges, Safe from all the
on the rock of a - ges, Safe from ev - 'ry storm,

93
storm that rag - es. Rich but not from
all the storm that rag - es. Rich in love, I'm rich,
G G/D G Am/G G/D G G/D G Am/G G/D Am/D
97
Sa - tan's wag - es, I'm stand - ing on the sol - id
not from Sa - tan's wag - es, I'm stand - ing on the sol - id
G G/D G/D D♯°7 Em G/D G/B Am/C G/D D7
101
rock. I'm stand - ing on the
rock. I'm stand-ing on the rock,
Bm7 E7 A N.C.

rock of a - ges, Safe _____ from all the
on the rock of a - ges, Safe from ev-'ry storm,

storm that rag - es. Rich _____ but not from
all the storm that rag - es. Rich in love, I'm rich,

51 | E F#m7 E/G# | A A/E | A Bm/A A/E Bm/E

Sa - tan's wag - es, I'm stand-ing on the sol - id
not from Sa - tan's wag - es, I'm stand-ing on the sol - id

A | A/E | A/E E#°7 F#m | A/E A/C# Bm/D A/E E#°7

rock. I'm stand-ing on the sol - id rock!

I Won't Have to Worry Anymore

Words and Music by
JIMMY JONES and JAMES GOSS
Arranged by Marty Hamby

Gospel Shuffle (♩ = 104)

Down here my burden's heavy, and the road seems rough and long. Some-

Copyright © 1971 Goss Brothers Music Co. (BMI) (adm. at ClearBox Rights, LLC). All rights reserved. Used by permission.

PLEASE NOTE: The copying of this music is prohibited by law and is not covered by CCLI or OneLicense.net.

times my feet get wear-y and so sore, But a bright-er day is com-ing, soon I'll step on heav-en's shore and I won't have to

Add MEN

wor - ry an - y - more._____ I won't have to wor - ry when I reach the oth - er shore, All my troub - les will be o - ver and I'll rest for-ev-er-more. My eyes will be on Je-sus and my heart will be a-glow And I won't have to wor-ry an-y-more.

Some day when life is over and I've said my last good-bye I'll see my Savior standing at the door. Then I'll hear Him say "You're wel-come, all your cares are left be-hind." And I won't have to wor-ry an-y-more. I won't have to

worry when I reach the oth-er shore, All my troub-les will be o-ver and I'll rest for-ev-er-more. My eyes will be on Je-sus and my heart will be a - glow And I won't have to wor - ry an - y - more._____ My eyes will be on Je - sus and my heart will be a -

glow And I won't have to wor-ry an-y-more, an-y-more, an-y-more.

Touring That City

Words and Music by
HAROLD LANE
Arranged by Marty Hamby

Son of God is the Light. You'll find me there on the streets so pretty, made of gold so pure and so bright with

Jesus the One, Who gave me the vict'ry, Who led me across the divide. Some morning you'll find me touring that city where with

122

[58] LADIES *unis.* *mf*

Him I will ev-er a-bide. Man-y times I have won-dered 'bout the sights of that cit-y, and all that my eyes shall be-hold; I will see all the won-ders when I en-ter that cit-y there for-ev-er to be safe in His fold. Some morn-ing you'll find me tour-ing that cit-y where the

Son of God is the Light. You'll find me there on the streets so pretty, made of gold so pure and so bright with

Chords: F | C | C/G | C | C/G | F/C C | D | D7 | G | G7

Je - sus the One, Who gave me the vic - t'ry, Who led me a - cross the di - vide. Some morn - ing you'll find me tour - ing that cit - y where with

Him I will ev - er a - bide. Here on earth we have trou - bles that to us seem so heav - y, but in heav - en no one will be sad; Mom and

Dad will be sing-ing, Heav-en's praise will be ring-ing for the dear-est Friend I ev-er had. Some morn-ing you'll find me tour-ing that cit-y where the

Son of God is the Light. You'll find me there on the streets so pret-ty, made of gold so pure and so bright with

Jesus the One, Who gave me the vict'ry, Who led me across the divide. Some morning you'll find me touring that city where with

Him I will ev-er a-bide. Some morn-ing you'll find me tour-ing that cit-y where the Son of God is the Light. You'll find me there on the streets so pret-ty, made of gold so pure and so bright with

Je-sus the One, Who gave me the vic-t'ry, Who led me a-cross the di-vide. Some

132

morn - ing you'll find me tour - ing that cit - y where with Him I will ev - er a - bide. Some morn - ing you'll find me tour - ing that cit - y where with

Him I will ev-er a-bide ___ I'll ev-er a-bide! ___

My God Is Real

Words and Music by
LOYCE MITCHELL and MRS. LUTHER M. HUTCHINS
Arranged by Marty Hamby

Majestic (♩ = 80)

Lyrics: My God is real, for I can feel Him in my

Copyright © 1979 Bridge Building Music (BMI) (adm. at CapitolCMGPublishing.com). All rights reserved. Used by permission.
PLEASE NOTE: The copying of this music is prohibited by law and is not covered by CCLI or OneLicense.net.

In four (♩. = 60)

FEMALE SOLO
mf

There are some soul. things I may not know, there are some

pla - ces I____ can't go. But__ I'm sure of this one thing____ that God is

real for I can feel Him deep with-in. _____ Yes, God is
real, _____ real in my soul. Yes, God is

CHOIR parts
Yes, God is real, real in my soul. _____

real, for He has washed and made me whole. His love for

For He has washed and made me whole.

F | Dm7 | G7 | C | G7 | C | Gm/C

me is like pure gold, Yes, God is

His love for me is like pure gold,

F | F+/A | B♭ | B°7

139

real, for I can feel Him in my soul.   *I can-not*

for I can feel Him in my soul.

tell just how you felt when Je- sus

140

took all your sins a-way. But since that day, and since that hour, God has been real, for I can feel His ho-ly pow'r. Yes, God is real, real in my soul. Yes, God is real, Yes, God is real, real in my soul.

36
real, for He has washed and made me whole. His love for
For He has washed and made me whole.
G Em7 A7 D A7 D C/D
38
me is like pure gold, Yes, God is
His love for me is like pure gold,
G G+/B C C#°7

143

68

real, for I can feel Him in my soul. Yes, God is

for I can feel Him in my soul.

G/D   D7sus   D7   G   Am7/G   G   G7/B

real,_____ real in my soul. Yes, God is

Yes, God is real, real in my soul._____

C   Am/C   G   C/G   G   D7sus

real, for He has washed and made me whole. His love for

For He has washed and made me whole.

me is like pure gold, Yes, God is

His love for me is like pure gold,

real, for I can feel Him in my soul. Yes, God is

for I can feel Him in my soul. Yes, God is

G/D　D7sus　D♯°7　Em　G7/D　C　Am7

Tempo I (♩ = 80)

rit.

real, for I can feel

real, for I can feel

G/D　G/B　Am/C　C6/D

Tempo I (♩ = 80)

rit.

146

That I Could Still Go Free

**Words and Music by
RONNY HINSON**
Arranged by Marty Hamby

Gospel Shuffle (♩=72)

Lock___ me up___ in a

Copyright © 1975 Stellar Pearls Publishing (BMI). All rights reserved. Used by permission.

PLEASE NOTE: The copying of this music is prohibited by law and is not covered by CCLI or OneLicense.net.

148

pris-on ___ and throw ___ a-way ___ the key, ___ Take ___ a-way ___ the vis-ion ___ from these eyes ___ that now can

149

see. De-prive____ me of the food____ I eat and e-ven__ bind my__ hands and my feet, but as long____ as I know

Je - sus, then I can still go free. That I could still go

CHOIR parts
That I could still go

free, _____ what kind _____ of Man would
free, _____ what kind _____ of Man would

F | C/E Dm7 C | C/G | F/G

reach out _____ His hand and do this for me? _____
reach out _____ His hand and do this for me? _____

C | C/G F/G | C G/B Am7 G

152

Oh, un-worth-y____ to ____ Yes, for me?____ Oo____

live, and not fit____ to kill, but then a Man on____ the

but then a Man on____ the

cross put me in His will and said that I could

cross put me in His will, and said that I could

still go free.

still go free.

154

MALE SOLO

Now I never could quite understand why a King would want to leave His throne to don the robe of an earthly

155

man, and feel the pain_____ of flesh and_____ bone.___ Then to lat - er trod that lone - ly path that led to

156

Cal - va - ry but those blood red stains, they broke all my chains and said that I could still go free.

MALE SOLO

That I could still go free,

CHOIR *parts*

That I could still go free,

what kind of Man would reach out His

what kind of Man would reach out His

158

hand and do this for me?

hand and do this for me? Yes, for

Oh, un-worth-y to live, and

me? Oo

not fit to kill, but then a Man on the cross put

but then a Man on the cross put

me in His will and said that I could still go

me in His will, and said that I could still go

free. That Man on the cross put

free. That Man on the cross put

me in His will and said that I could

me in His will, and said that I could

still go free.

still go free, I could go free.

Thank God I am free!

Thank God, I am free!